Rabbits and Rats, Birds and Seeds, Cactus and Trees

Plants and animals at work in
El Pinacate, Sonoran Desert, Mexico

by Renaldo, as told to Paul Dayton

Dedicated to the people of Mexico
for supporting
El Pinacate, a Biosphere Reserve and a World Heritage Site,
and to Carlos Castillo and Federico Godínez Leal
and all the Park personnel
for their wonderful management of this world treasure

Copyright © 2017 Paul Dayton
Drawings © 2017 Susan Heller
Photographs by Paul Dayton and others as noted
Cover landscape: Jimmy Fumo

All rights reserved. Except for brief excerpts used in the context of a review, contact the publisher for permission to reproduce any part of this book.

Dayton Publishing LLC
Solana Beach, CA 92075
publisher@daytonpublishing.com
www.daytonpublishing.com

ISBN: 978-0997003253

We wish to thank the photographers who have generously allowed us to use their photos in this book. Their names appear beside their photos.

Contents

Hello, My Name Is Renaldo 1

Rain 2

Cholla and Rain 3

Cholla, Rain and Packrats 5

Ocotillo, Jackrabbits and Cholla 8

Saguaros and "Nurse Trees" 15

Saguaros, Nurse Trees and Mistletoe 18

Saguaros, Nurse Trees, Packrats and Infection 21

Jackrabbits, Saguaros and Rain 23

Now You Know 27

Hello, my name is Renaldo.

I am a Sonoran *desert tortoise,* and I live in *El Pinacate and Gran Desierto de Altar Biosphere Reserve,* a UNESCO World Heritage Site in Sonora, Mexico. I am more than 80 years old, and I've lived here all my life. I want to tell you about some of the things I've seen.

Rain

When you live as long as I have, you see many kinds of weather. Sometimes there are long dry periods, called *droughts*. in summer, short bursts of heavy rains, called *monsoons*, soak the desert soil. And during some winters, weather conditions we call *El Niño* can bring long periods of rain.

All plants and animals need water to live. In a desert, like El Pinacate, water is scarce. So the rain, when it comes, is really important for desert life. After the rain, plants and animals can grow again, and the dry desert landscape changes.

This is what it looks like when rain comes to El Pinacate after a long drought.

Cholla and Rain

Take a look at the *jumping cholla*. It's a very spiny cactus, and it can survive long periods without rain. As you can imagine, this cactus isn't my favorite food — it's covered with sharp spines!

But I'm lucky, because when the weather is really dry and not many other plants can grow, I can eat the cholla, spines and all. Not many other animals can do that.

The jumping cholla looks fuzzy from a distance, but its spines are sharp!

The jumping cholla doesn't make seeds to start new cholla plants. Instead, it drops "buds" from the ends of its branches. Not the kind of buds that turn into flowers, just little round pieces of cactus.

Gusts of wind blow some of these cholla buds along the ground. *If* a bud ends up in a place where it can send roots down into the ground, and *if* the roots can get enough water, and *if* the bud doesn't get eaten, it will grow. A few of the cholla buds survive and grow to be big chollas that make buds of their own.

The number of buds a cholla can make depends on the rainfall. After a period of good soaking rains, a cholla can produce a large crop of buds. But it may take a year or two after the rain for the buds to appear.

Round "buds" fall from the ends of cholla branches.

Some of the cholla buds take root and grow.

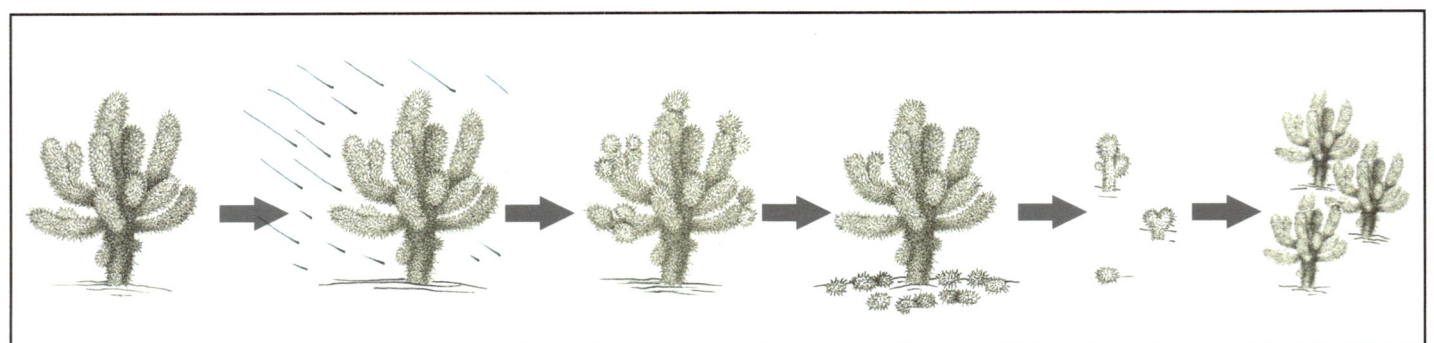

After a soaking rain, chollas make buds that fall off, are blown by the wind and may grow to make more chollas.

Cholla, Rain and Packrats

Now that you know how cholla grow, I'll tell you — we desert tortoises are not the only animals that eat cholla buds. *Packrats* eat them too.

Packrats carry their cactus buds home to large nests, called *middens*. At first glance, a midden can look pretty messy. But it's a useful mess.

Packrats eat only the fleshy parts of the cholla buds. They don't eat the spines the way I do. Instead they use those sharp parts for protection. They put spines, and sometimes even whole buds, on top of their middens and in front of the entrances. Coyotes, bobcats and other predators stay away — they don't want to risk stepping on the sharp-spined cholla.

Packrats gather cholla buds for food and to defend their middens.

Packrats come out of their homes to look for cholla buds and other food at night, when it's dark. That's because coyotes, bobcats, badgers and foxes like to eat any smaller animals they can catch. And many of these predators are out looking for prey in the daytime.

Even at night, coming out into the open is risky, because owls like to eat packrats too. So at night the packrats run fast from one bush to another. They hide in places shaded from moonlight, and they pick up cholla buds the wind has blown under the bushes. As you walk around the desert in the daytime, you can see the trails packrats leave behind when they search for food.

At night packrats run from bush to bush to avoid owls, leaving "trails" we can see in the daytime.

Do you remember? A year or two after a good rainy period the chollas start producing many buds. Well, when that happens, the packrats have plenty to eat. They get fat and healthy, so they can have lots of babies. Soon there may be four or five times as many packrats as there were before the rains. And they're not leaving many cholla buds for desert tortoises to eat.

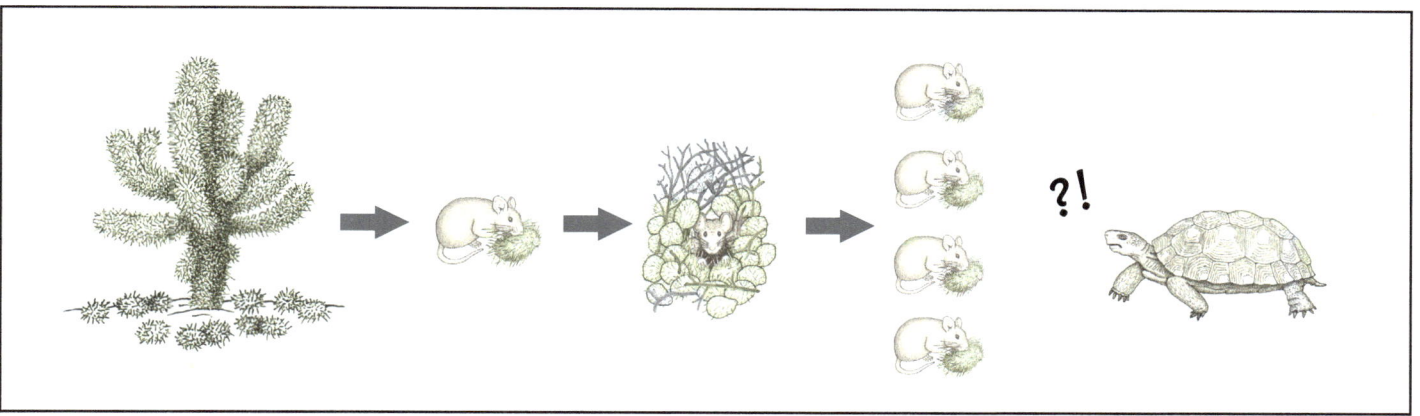

When there's plenty of cholla, soon there are lots more packrats. They eat up most of the cholla buds, and then it's harder to find food.

Ocotillo, Jackrabbits and Cholla

Besides feeding animals like me and the packrats, the cholla also helps certain plants survive. One of these plants is the *ocotillo*.

When an ocotillo is in bloom, its long green, leaf-covered "arms" are capped with red flowers. Underneath the green leaves, the long ocotillo arms have woody "stems."

When water is plentiful, the ocotillo's woody stems are covered with green leaves. There are fewer leaves in dry times (inset).

But the young ocotillo arms are different. They're small and tender and not woody at all. At this stage, some desert animals, such as the *black-tailed jackrabbit*, can eat them.

Deer, cattle and sheep also eat young ocotillo branches. But in El Pinacate the black-tailed jackrabbits eat the most.

The young, reddish shoots you see here are tender and easy to chew.

Black-tailed jackrabbits can eat the tender young ocotillo stems.

If you see jackrabbit poo on the ground around the bottom of an ocotillo, it's a sure sign jackrabbits have been munching the new, tender ocotillo arms. And if you look closely at the very bottom of an ocotillo, you might be able to see where new arms were chewed off while they were still small and soft. While the new branches around the base of an ocotillo are being eaten off, the branches in the center have a chance to grow tall and woody.

Some ocotillos show "scars" or woody stubs where jackrabbits have chewed off new, tender growth.

Jackrabbits can't eat woody branches. When a jackrabbit-chewed ocotillo gets big, it may have only a few arms left, growing almost straight up. Ocotillos that weren't chewed so much by jackrabbits look different. Instead they have many shorter arms that extend outward from the base of the plant.

Some ocotillos have a "bushy" shape. Others have fewer stems, maybe because a jackrabbit ate the outer arms of the young plant.

The red flowers of the ocotillo wave like flags at the ends of the woody stems. Hummingbirds and moths are attracted to the flowers and drink the sugary nectar inside them. A dusting of pollen "hitches a ride" on the nectar drinkers. They carry the pollen from ocotillo to ocotillo so the flowers can make seeds. Some seeds fall directly to the ground. Others are carried away, or *dispersed*, by the wind.

The bright red flowers on the ends of the ocotillo branches attact flying pollinators like this hummingbird sipping nectar.

A few of the ocotillo seeds land in places where they can sprout. If they do start to grow, many of the new plants are eaten right away while they are very little and soft.

A young ocotillo has a better chance of surviving if it is protected by a cholla. If an ocotillo seed sprouts next to a cholla, the cactus's spines can protect the small, tender plant from being eaten by animals like the jackrabbit.

As the ocotillo gets bigger, its branches become tough and woody, so it doesn't need as much protection anymore. But the ocotillo now needs more water. Its roots grow big, and they start to compete with the cholla roots, taking the water the cholla needs to live.

A cholla protects a young ocotillo.

A protected ocotillo grows. Its roots compete with the cholla's roots to get water from the ground.

Sometimes the ocotillo outlives the cholla that protected it.

Eventually the cholla that protected the young plants may die because it can't get enough water. The ocotillo, now big and tough, continues to grow in its place. After a while termites eat the woody skeleton of the dead cholla, or it rots in the strong desert sunlight.

Unless you have watched for a long time, as I have, you might not understand: When you see an ocotillo, there may once have been a cholla growing next to it. The cholla made it possible for the ocotillo to survive until its arms grew tough enough to resist black-tailed jackrabbits.

If an ocotillo seed lands under a cholla, the cholla may protect the young plant from the jackrabbit. The growing ocotillo competes with the cholla for water, and the cholla may die as a result.

Saguaros and "Nurse Trees"

Do you think there might be other plants, besides the ocotillo, that could use help when they're small? If you think so, you're right! One of those plants is the *saguaro* cactus.

In early summer, if there has been enough rain, saguaros make large white flowers, mostly at the ends of their main "trunk" and their "arms." The flowers attract bats, which visit at night to eat their nectar. During these visits, the bats pick up pollen on their fur. As the bats travel from cactus to cactus, the pollen gets carried along, fertilizing other saguaro flowers to make seeds.

Saguaros in El Pinacate desert

White saguaro flowers attract bats, which pollinate the cactus.

After its seeds are fertilized, the saguaro makes fruit. The fruits split open to show sweet black pulp that's full of seeds, surrounded by red that attracts birds. When birds eat the pulp, they don't digest the seeds. Often, when the birds have had a good meal of cactus fruit, they fly off to rest in a nearby tree. While they sit there, they poop, or *defecate*. Seeds fall to the ground under the tree. That's why many saguaros germinate beneath trees, very often palo verde, mesquite or ironwood trees.

Saguaro flowers produce fruits that are red when they open.   *The fruit splits open, showing the black pulp inside.*

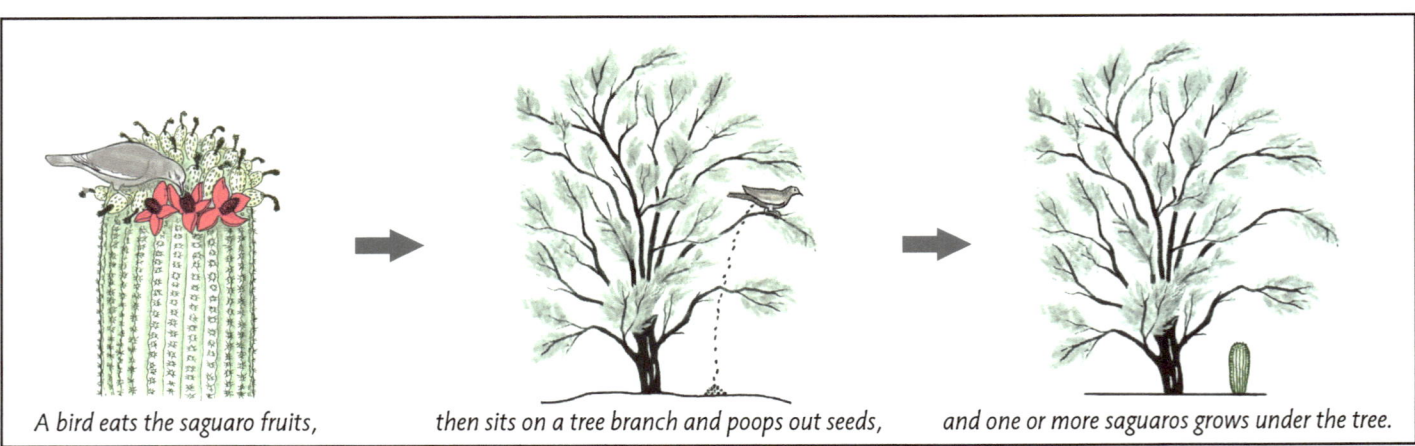

A bird eats the saguaro fruits,   *then sits on a tree branch and poops out seeds,*   *and one or more saguaros grows under the tree.*

These *"nurse trees"* protect the small saguaro plants from freezing in the winter and from too much sun in the summer. Also, when the leaves of these trees fall to the ground, they bring nutrients to the soil, nutrients the saguaro needs to grow. If you look around El Pinacate, you can see many examples of a saguaro and its nurse tree living together. But eventually, that relationship is likely to change.

A nurse tree protects a young saguaro cactus.

A nurse tree and a saguaro share the space as the cactus grows.

Saguaros, Nurse Trees and Mistletoe

Like so many things that happen in El Pinacate, what happens next with a saguaro and its nurse tree depends on water.

Palo verde, *mesquite* and *ironwood* trees have deep root systems that can find water far underground. But these trees also depend on roots near the surface that collect rainwater.

The saguaro's roots don't go deep. Their shallow roots are good at absorbing rainwater at the surface, before a nearby tree can get it.

When it rains, if the saguaro takes almost all of the rain water, its nurse tree is stressed. And that's where *mistletoe* comes in.

Mesquite, ironwood and palo verde trees have both deep and shallow roots.

Saguaro roots spread out near the surface.

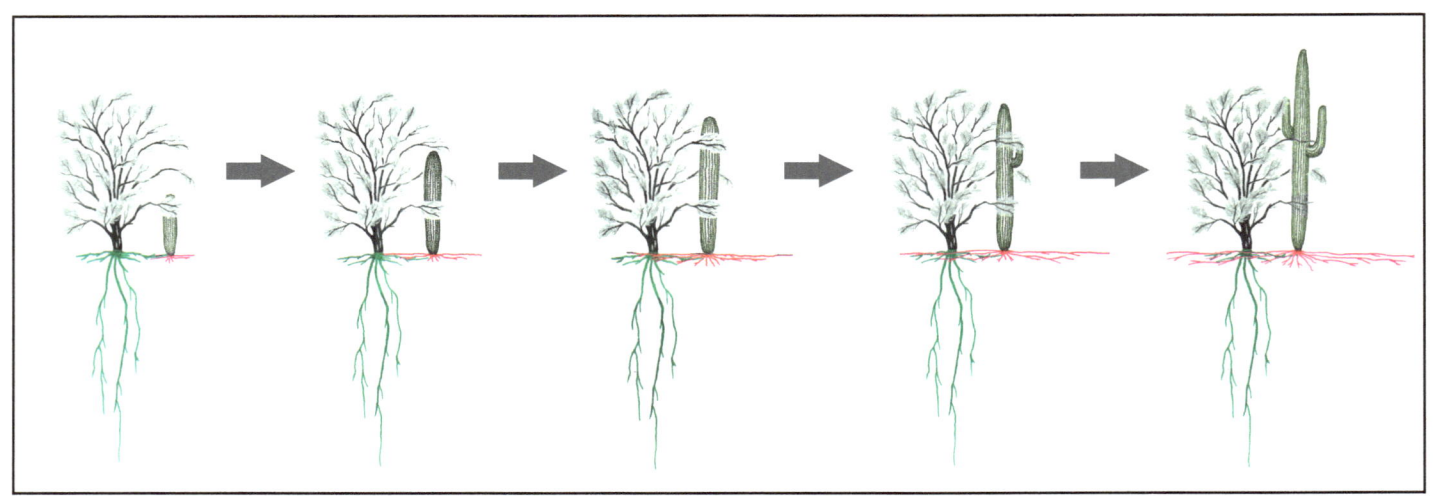

As a protected saguaro grows, its roots grow too. They spread out and compete with the nurse tree's roots for rainwater at the surface.

Mistletoe is a *parasite* plant. That means it steals water and nutrients from a *host,* the plant it lives on.

Mistletoe spreads from tree to tree when a bird eats the berries of a mistletoe plant, then lands on a nearby tree and defecates the sticky seeds onto its branches.

Each seed produces a small root that tries to penetrate the branch. A healthy tree has sap that can push the mistletoe root back out of the branch before it can grow and steal water and nutrients. But what if the tree is already stressed because a saguaro is competing for the tree's water? The stressed tree can't produce as much sap, and it's easier for the mistletoe root to penetrate. So it can steal water and nutrients and begin to grow.

Birds eat mistletoe berries and spread the seeds to other nearby trees.

Sticky mistletoe seeds land on a branch of the host tree and grow roots to penetrate the tree.

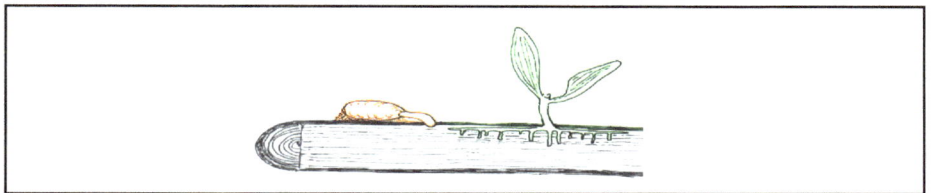

New mistletoe plants begins to grow from the seeds that have penetrated the tree.

Once mistletoe starts growing on the tree, the mistletoe plant uses the water and nutrients it steals to grow branches and make berries. Birds eat the berries and defecate more seeds onto the nurse tree's branches. The stressed tree can't defend itself against all these seeds. And soon the tree is full of mistletoe, adding to the stress.

Eventually, the nurse tree might lose so much of its water and nutrients that it dies. When the nurse tree dies, the mistletoe dies too, of course, because it can no longer get water and nutrients from the tree. But if the saguaro is big and strong when the tree dies, the saguaro survives.

After a while the dead tree falls over, and the cactus stands alone. When you see a lone saguaro in El Pinacate, or a group of saguaros close together, remember that the cactus might have had a nurse tree once, that helped it get started.

Once the mistletoe grows and makes berries, birds eat them and more mistletoe plants grow on the tree.

When mistletoe gets started on a nurse tree, it can spread and take over, especially if the tree is weak because of competition for water.